NOAH'S ARK

words by Roger McGough
pictures by Ljiljana Rylands

Published by Dinosaur Publications

It began
When God popped His head
Through the clouds and said:

"Oh you wicked, wicked children
What a mess this place is in
All the violence and corruption
It really is a sin.

I turn my back for five aeons
(For I've other work to do)
Keeping the universe tidy
And I get no thanks from you.

You've grown selfish and conceited
Your manners are a disgrace
You come and go just as you please
You'd think you owned the place.

A telling-off's not good enough
You've grown too big for your flesh
So I think I'll wash my hands of you
And start again afresh."

He turned full on the tap in the sky
Then picked out the one good man
Pure of heart and strong in arm
To carry out His plan: Noah.

"What I need," explained God
"Is an arkwright to build an ark, right away."
Said Noah, "If I can sir."
"Of course you can, now get stuck in
I won't take Noah for an answer."

"I want a boat three storeys high
Aboard which you will bring
Not only your wife and family
But two of every living thing."

"Even spiders?" asked Noah
(who didn't really like them)
"Even spiders," said God
(who didn't either).

"Cats and dogs and elephants
Slugs, leopards and lice
Giraffes and armadilloes
Buffaloes, bed bugs and mice.

Antelopes, ants and anteaters
(though keep those last two apart)
Bears from Koala to Grizzly
Horses from Racing to Cart.

Fish will be able to fend for themselves
And besides, a wooden ark
Is not the sort of place to keep
A whale or an angry shark.

And don't forget our feathered friends
For they'll have nowhere to nest.
But vermin will determine
Their own survival best.

Flies, maggots and bluebottles
Mosquitoes and stingers that bite
Will live off the dead and the dying
So they'll make out all right.

That seems to be all for now, Noah
The rest is up to you
I'll see you again in forty days
Until then God Bless and Adieu."

He disappeared in a clap of thunder
(Either that or he banged the door)
And the wind in a rage broke out of its cage
With an earth-splintering roar.

And no sooner was everyone aboard
Than the Ark gave a mighty shudder
And would have been crushed by the onrushing waves
Had Noah not been at the rudder.

Right craftily he steered the craft
As if to the mariner born
Through seas as high as a Cyclop's eye
And cold as the devil's spawn.

And it rained, and it rained
And it rained again
And it rained, and it rained
And it rained, and then . . .
             . . . drip . . .
      . . . drop . . .
      . . . the last . . .
      . . . drip dropped . . .
             . . . to a . . .

. . . stop.

Noah at the helm was overwhelmed
For both cargo and crew were unharmed
Then the wind turned nasty and held its breath
So the Ark became becalmed.

Hither and thither it drifted
Like an aimless piece of jetsam
"Food's running out," cried Mrs Noah
"We'll perish if we don't get some."

"Maybe God's gone and forgotten us
We're alone in the world and forsaken
He surely won't miss one little pig
Shall I grill a few rashers of bacon?"

"Naughty, naughty!" said Noah sternly
(For it was the stern that he was stood in)
"I'm ravenous, but bring me a raven
I've an idea and I think it's a good 'un."

As good as his word, he let loose the bird
"Go spy out for land," he commanded
But in less than a week, it was back with its beak
Completely (so to speak) empty-handed!

Next he coaxed from its lovenest a dove
"We're depending on you," he confided
Then gave it to the air like an unwrapped gift
Of white paper, that far away glided.

Then the Ark sat about with its heart in its mouth
With nothing to do but wait
So Mrs Noah organised organised games
To keep animal minds off their fate.

Until one morn when all seemed lost
The dove in the heavens was seen
To the Ark, like an archangel it arrowed
Bearing good tidings of green.

"Praised be the Lord," cried Noah
(and Mrs Noah cried too)
And all God's creatures gave their thanks
(even spiders, to give them their due).

Then God sent a quartet of rainbows
Radiating one from each side
To the four corners of the earth
Where they journeyed and multiplied.

And as Noah set off down the mountain
To be a simple farmer again
A voice thundered: "Nice work there sunshine."
Here endeth the story. Amen.

Published by Dinosaur Publications
8 Grafton Street, London W1X 3LA

Dinosaur Publications is an imprint of
Fontana Paperbacks, part of the
Collins Publishing Group

Printed by Warners of Bourne and London